Contents

SOLD

Morning

I am a busy kid!

My body needs fuel.

I eat well.

I eat breakfast.

Yogurt has protein.

It fills me up.

Dad adds nuts.

I add berries.

Snack time!

I peel a banana.

Fruit has vitamins.

They help my body grow.

Afternoon

Lunchtime!

We eat pasta.

We drink milk.

Green salad has minerals.

I eat a snack after school.

Carrots fill me up.

Football!

I drink lots of water.

Water keeps me cool.

Evening

Let's cook dinner!

I cut a tomato with Mum.

My brother grates cheese.

We eat chicken wraps.

Mmm!

I love sweet food.

But dessert is a rare treat.

Tasty!

Good food helps
my body grow.
Eating well means
a healthy me!

Glossary

dessert   a sweet food eaten at the end of a meal

mineral   a substance the body needs; iron and calcium are minerals.

protein   something in food that the body uses to build and repair itself; meat, nuts and beans are high in protein.

rare   not often seen, found or happening

vitamin   tiny bits inside food that the body needs; Vitamin D helps bones; Vitamin A helps eyes.

yogurt   a thick food made from milk

Find out more

Books

Choose Good Food!: My Eating Tips, Gina Bellisario (Millbrook Press, 2014)

Eating Well (Take Care of Yourself!), Sian Smith (Raintree, 2013)

Healthy Eating (Let's Read and Talk About), Honor Head (Franklin Watts, 2014)

Websites

kidshealth.org/en/kids/stay-healthy/
Find lots of information and tips on eating healthily.

www.bbc.co.uk/education/clips/zrd4d2p
Songs and videos teach you about healthy eating.

www.bbc.co.uk/northernireland/schools/4_11/uptoyou/
Discover fun games to remind you to eat healthy food.

Comprehension questions

1. What does yogurt contain?

2. Why is it important to drink water?

3. Greens contain minerals.
   What is a mineral?

Index